AWAKEN HOPE

Reflections on the Season of Advent

⟡ LIFE **TEEN**

Designed by David Calavitta and Casey Olson.

Copy editing by Elizabeth Bayardi and Rachel Peñate.

Authored by Brittany Calavitta, Leah Murphy, Rachel Peñate, Joel Stepanek, and Jason Theobald.

Published by Life Teen, Inc.
2222 S. Dobson Rd. Suite 601
Mesa, AZ 85202
LifeTeen.com

Printed in the United States of America. Printed on acid-free paper.

INTRODUCTION

Jason Theobald

As a young kid, I loved sports. In fact, my first word was "ball," and I loved the excitement that came from playing. So, as a very enthusiastic first grader, I happily picked up the game of baseball. Anyone who has watched baseball knows this though: there can be large chunks of time in between when the player runs out to his post in the outfield and a ball actually comes to him. In the midst of this waiting, I was that kid. The one you will quite often see in the outfield of a little league game: I was picking grass, watching the parents on the sidelines, and every once in awhile, completely abandoning my post to go use the port-a-potty.

When I look back on those days of little league, I think about the embarrassment of my mom pulling me off the field because she could tell seven-year-old me needed to use the bathroom and I realize there was one trait of a great baseball player that I was lacking as a child: focus. In order to stand in one place for an extended period of time, watch plays that don't involve you, and then spring into action exactly when you're called upon, you need an intense ability to focus. You need to choose that the task at hand is worth giving your all to, and then you need to put your heart, your mind, and all of your effort into that thing.

Advent sometimes feels like it comes really quickly. Fall happens, and we're surrounded with pumpkins and lattes. Then before we know it, we're thinking about our Christmas presents and time off from school. It is incredibly easy to get caught up in the chaos of this season and have our minds wandering in a million different directions.

The Psalm for the First Sunday in Advent this year, coming from Psalm 80, says this:

Lord, make us turn to you; let us see your face and we shall be saved.

What if – unlike me in the outfield, back in my little league days – we really focused this Advent? What if, as the Psalmist here says, we truly turned our face to the Lord? As children playing in the outfield, this focus is difficult, if not impossible; as we seek to grow in our faith, however, this focus becomes not only possible, but necessary.

There is so much happening in Advent. None of the things we do in this season are bad; in fact, all of them point to the reality that these four weeks are a time of preparation, and what a beautiful thing it is we are preparing for! In a mere number of days, we are going to celebrate the fact that the God of space and time entered into our fallen world as a baby born in a manger to a poor virgin, named Mary, and her husband, Joseph. In a few short weeks, we will remember the night when all of space and time stood still and turned to look at a crying baby, and in His face saw the redemption of all mankind.

I can only speak for myself, but I can say with certainty that as I string that garland so neatly around the banner in my house, I'm not always reflecting on the fact that without the events of Christmas, I would not be able to have an intimate, personal relationship with God the Father. I have gone to plenty of Christmas parties without once pausing to reflect on the fact that the Father spared His Son, who was born in a cave because there was no room for Him, so that I might not be dead in my sin any longer.

This Advent, maybe what can be different is our focus. What would the singing of "Silent Night" at that Christmas Eve Mass mean to us if, for the last four weeks, we had been intensely focused on the reality that the Savior was about to come and meet us in our brokenness on that very Silent Night?

Over the next four weeks, as our hearts are torn in a million different directions in the busyness of the season, don't let your focus stray from the scene of the nativity. If each one of us, in a real and authentic way, sought to enter into the silence, the beauty, and the joy of that moment, Christmas would bring new meaning to our lives as well as the lives of those around us.

These reflections on the season of Advent are here to help you enter into this season, turn towards Christ, and truly focus; not to focus on the externals, but instead be moved by this time to truly encounter the Lord in our waiting and in the exultant celebration which comes at Christmas. May this season truly be a joyful time for you as you pause and focus your heart on Emmanuel, God with us, who longs to come, not just in general, but in a real and specific way into the hearts that invite Him.

Happy Advent, friends. May our hearts be focused on Jesus, born of the Virgin, for whom we wait.

THE POWER OF PEACE

The First Week of Advent

December 3 - 9

Leah Murphy

THE FIRST SUNDAY OF ADVENT

Sunday, December 3rd

Isaiah 63:16b-17, 19b; 64:2-7
Psalm 80:2-3, 15-16, 18-19
1 Corinthians 1:3-9
Mark 13:33-37

I'm a shameless cradle Catholic. I was baptized as a little baby and grew up in the Church, usually pretty eager at every point of growth and development to know and love Jesus more. That said, I'd become quite familiar with the phrase, "God will satisfy the desires of your heart." I'd like to think that, at some point, I really believed it, but I can't honestly say that I always did.

Growing up, I thought that I had control over every aspect of my life. I would work hard to do well in school. I would act responsibly so that I could acquire leadership positions. I would take the right classes to advance towards a job that could turn into the career that I wanted. So whenever any of those things that I was controlling would become out of reach, I would doubt God's faithfulness. Whenever things weren't going exactly as I planned, I'd question Him: "You're supposed to satisfy the desires of my heart, but you're taking this opportunity or relationship away from me? How can I trust You?" I couldn't believe that surrendering to His plan would bring me any real joy or peace because it was beyond what I could see, so I kept chasing after the false peace that came with controlling everything I could.

It wasn't until I lost control over every aspect of my life that I started to see the goodness of God's presence in my life unfold. I don't mean this "loss of control" in some kind of dramatic, rock bottom, devastating way, but rather in the sense that things weren't going according to plan – I didn't have all the things in life that I wanted. And in that moment, I had two choices: chase after the things that I wanted or surrender to Jesus, clinging to Him and Him alone.

For about three years, I chose to chase after everything I wanted. I tried grasping for the careers, the success, and the relationships I believed would make me happy, but they led me nowhere. I found myself more isolated and lonely than ever, constantly looking to something else to make me happy, and finding peace nowhere.

After the relationship that I wanted fell apart, after all my plans as I'd articulated them didn't come to fruition, and after realizing how empty a life without Jesus was, I gave up. In a reluctant (and rather bratty) prayer during my early twenties, I journaled to Jesus along the lines of, "You're apparently all that's left. I can't seem to make things work on my own, and I'm tired of trying, so Your move."

And He did move. With that tiny bit of faith I was able to surrender, He was able to lead me to the truest reality I've ever known:

that He does indeed satisfy the desires of my heart with His own heart. And it was in that surrender that I found true peace – a peace that allowed me to really believe He was enough, and this peace freed me from spending my life chasing it anywhere else.

Today, we enter into my all-time favorite liturgical season, Advent. With this season comes so much joy, peaceful anticipation, Advent wreaths, and, apart from the liturgical realities, the world is suddenly full of mistletoe-scented candles, Christmas lights, and cozy, peppermint mocha weather.

While this season is often known as a season of waiting for the Christ-child, it's also a profoundly beautiful invitation to reacquaint ourselves with the peace that Jesus, and Jesus alone, can give when we surrender to Him.

In today's First Reading, Isaiah prays to God, acknowledging Israel's penchant for wandering away from Him. He demands the answer to the question, "Why do you let us wander, o Lord, from your ways and harden our hearts so that we fear You not?" (Isaiah 63:17). The prophet begs for God to return, to come in powerful signs and awesome deeds, to help the Israelite people amend their ways. But his raw and honest prayer for Israel ends with a profound, peaceful surrender to Him: "O Lord, You are our Father; we are the clay and you are the potter: we are all the work of your hands" (Isaiah 64:7).

It's that final admission of the need for a Savior that ushers us, most perfectly, into this season. As we light the first candle on the wreath, we are invited to echo Isaiah's prayer of surrender. Peace was all that Isaiah wanted for wayward Israel. The peace of union with God was all that the people of Israel wanted for themselves. But that peace is not attained by wandering from God or by putting conditions or expectations on His ability to save. *Peace comes by surrendering to the will of God and allowing the Messiah's coming, the reality of the Incarnation, to be enough to satisfy our hearts.*

Further Reflection: Consider one desire in your life that you are trying to achieve on your own and are unwilling to surrender to Jesus. Like the prophet Isaiah, be bold enough to surrender; to acknowledge that, as hard as you might try, you cannot be your own savior, and you need the Incarnate God, the person of Jesus, to fulfill the desires of your heart. Let go of your desire to bring about your own peace and allow Him to give it to you.

MONDAY OF THE FIRST WEEK OF ADVENT

Monday, December 4ᵗʰ

Matthew 8:5-11

Do you ever binge watch a series on Netflix and find yourself getting to an episode that's "full of necessary plot developments," but lacks any real action? No? Just me? Ok, well here's the deal: sometimes TV series will have a few episodes that lay the groundwork for future major plot points, but getting through those episodes can be rather boring because they lack any major action or drama.

Sometimes, that's how Jesus works. I'm not saying Jesus is boring because He's the furthest thing from that. But, more often than not, the way He works in our lives is not dramatic, but rather incredibly peaceful. And being open to His work in our lives requires incredible humility and great faith.

The centurion in today's Gospel is our example of this humility and faith. When Jesus responds to his request to heal his servant by asking to enter his home to cure him, the servant responds, "Lord, I am not worthy to have you enter under my roof; only say the word and my servant will be healed" (Matthew 8:6). Jesus is stunned by this response – the Gospel says that He was "amazed" at the centurion's faith. Although the centurion was asking God for a miracle, He didn't demand that God work in a showy way, having Him enter his house and heal his servant on the spot – He trusted that Jesus could work in ways beyond his understanding.

Is that your response to God's desire to enter into relationship with you at every Mass in receiving the Eucharist? Do we recognize Jesus' divinity – He is God and we are not, by our own capabilities, worthy of receiving Him. Yet at the same time, do we acknowledge that God is able to work miracles in our lives, even in the most peaceful, less dramatic ways? Even in the reception of this tiny miraculous white host?

Jesus is able to work in peaceful ways that are beyond our understanding. He does work miracles, but these miracles don't demand great circumstances, they simply require great humility and faith.

Further Reflection: As you prepare your heart to receive Jesus the next time you attend Mass, ask Him to reveal how He desires to move in peaceful, subtle ways in your life. He is no doubt working miracles, but, more often than not, it can feel more like a plot developing season of a TV series than an action packed episode.

TUESDAY OF THE FIRST WEEK OF ADVENT

Tuesday, December 5th

Luke 10:21-24

If you were to look up the word "power," it doesn't, by definition, qualify itself as a good or bad thing. Yet, it seems to often bear a somewhat aggressive connotation, especially in socio-political conversations. I'm thinking of Kanye West's lyrics, "no one man should have all that power," or every history lesson I've heard on the U.S. government's system of checks and balances needed to maintain a "separation of powers."

Yet we believe in an all-powerful God, Him who invades Earth by way of the Incarnation. Jesus is the Messiah that Israel had been waiting for – the great force that would finally unite them back to God and one another. And in today's Gospel acclamation we hear, "Our Lord shall come with power; He will enlighten the eyes of His servants."

Yet the power that Jesus comes with is one of peace that the world has never known. It is the power that favors justice for the poor (Isaiah 11), rescues the poor, and pities the lowly (Psalm 72). It is the power that is understood by the childlike, but not the wise and the learned (Luke 10).

Jesus' Incarnation – His taking on human flesh that He might die on a cross for our sake – is the ultimate act of power that the world will ever know. Yet it's in this unexpected, upside-down reality, where power is lived out in humble service of the poor, lonely, and forgotten, and is identified by peace. This means that we, as Christians, have to live according to a power that looks very different from the world's.

We are called to live out the Incarnation, and that means not being satisfied with the world's definitions of power or peace. It means forming relationships with the poorest people you encounter in your day-to-day life. It means risking your reputation to be a friend to the most judged or forgotten person at your school. It means not waiting for a political system to be set up to help foreigners gain access to basic human needs, but making yourself available to serve and support them, your neighbors, in any way that you're reasonably able. This peaceful power doesn't require a trust in worldly systems, but a surrendering to the will of God, Who is wholly good and loving.

Further Reflection: Take some time to reflect on how you can serve someone in need this week. Use the suggestions listed at the end of this reflection as a starting point.

WEDNESDAY OF THE FIRST WEEK OF ADVENT

Wednesday, December 6ᵗʰ

Matthew 15:29-37

You know how in superhero movies, there's always an odious villain? That one who, throughout almost the entire movie, keeps escaping destruction? And then, at the end of the story, you see the hero of the film finally take down this nemesis once and for all in an explosive scene full of action and excitement? The hero, in those moments, is often painted as an incredibly powerful, strong, formidable force. Rarely, is this hero ever portrayed as a quiet, gentle being. We, the audience, behold that hero in awe of his or her profound strength and power.

In the great superhero story of life (cheesy, I know, but go with me here), our hero, God, defeats our enemy, death, a little differently – not by some impressive display of strength, but by taking on our humanity and conquering it for Himself. We first behold Him, not as some strong, overwhelming force, but as a human baby – small, dependent, and vulnerable.

In today's First Reading, the prophet Isaiah describes this moment – the coming of the Messiah on the holy mountain of the Lord – telling Israel that on this mountain, God will destroy death forever and "on that day it will be said: 'Behold our God, to whom we looked; let us rejoice and be glad that He has saved us!'" (Isaiah 25:9). But the way we are introduced to our hero is far from what we expect, rather than looking up to an impressive figure full of power, we first behold a tiny baby in the arms of the Blessed Mother. And the moment when death is defeated is not a hero's moment – on a cross – instead we behold a man, brutally nailed to a cross. And now we behold our Lord, our hero, the great defeater of death, in a tiny white host.

God decided to make Himself small and invade our earthly reality in a peaceful way, and this is how He pursues us. He doesn't need a flashy scene to be held as a hero. Today, behold Him for what He is: the truest hero who brings with Him the truest peace.

Further Reflection: Consider how Jesus is pursuing you and your heart in your day-to-day life. Reflect on the peaceful advances He makes towards your heart, and behold Him and the power of His peace in those moments. Receive the subtle acts of love He gives you through other people. Notice His heroism in the simplicity of receiving or adoring the Eucharist. Invite Him into the wounds in your heart and receive the gentle, but overwhelming fullness of His healing mercy through Reconciliation.

MEMORIAL OF ST. AMBROSE, BISHOP AND DOCTOR OF THE CHURCH

Thursday, December 7th

Matthew 7:21, 24-27

Do you ever look back on a moment in life and (quite dramatically) think, "Wow I can't really believe I made it out of that alive!" Since I'm wildly dramatic, this moment for me happened during my senior year of college. I had two part-time jobs, was student body president, was trying to figure out what I was going to do after graduation, was trying to maintain a perfect GPA, and all while going through a pretty scary family crisis. Sometimes I look back at that phase and really wonder how I didn't fall apart under the weight of all of that; and I know that to some of you, that might sound like a patch of daisies compared to what you have struggled through. I honestly look back at that phase of great chaos and come to one conclusion: the peace that only Jesus can give is the sole reason I was able to sustain such chaos and not completely crumble.

In today's Gospel, we hear Jesus' teaching about the wise man who built his house on a rock, whose house was unharmed even during the most tempestuous of storms. According to Jesus, this man is the image of what it is to hear and act on His words about the Kingdom of Heaven. The most notable element about this teaching, in my opinion, is the fact that, regardless of what this man built his house on, the storm still comes – it's inevitable. Yet, he's able to maintain the peace of keeping a roof over his head because, although the house is shaken, it's not destroyed.

And that is the key of what it is to trust in Jesus' teachings: we'll still face challenges and we may even be shaken, but if our trust is in Him, we will not be destroyed. Peace can remain.

Further Reflection: If you're struggling through a stormy period of life right now or if you can look back on one, I challenge you to reflect on where you are or have been putting your trust. Don't pretend that you won't face challenges simply because you've received Jesus into your life, but don't be deceived into thinking that He isn't more powerful than those challenges. His peace will remain if you let it be your foundation.

SOLEMNITY OF THE IMMACULATE CONCEPTION OF THE BLESSED VIRGIN MARY

Friday, December 8th

Luke 1:26-38

We take a break from our normal broadcast to bring you this special report: the Mother of God, Mary, daughter of Sts. Anne and Joachim, was conceived without sin. Yes, we're still in the season of Advent, and yes, we're nearing the birth of our Lord and Savior, Jesus Christ; but today, in a special way, we celebrate the conception of Mary, that very Lord and Savior's mother.

This is a reality the Church celebrates today, not only because Mary was some incredibly amazing human being who never fell into sin, but because God is an incredible God, who, through a one time act of grace, allowed Mary to be conceived without original sin. First and foremost, this day is about honoring the way God's grace made it possible for Mary to say "yes" to the Incarnation, to have a faith big enough to say to the angel, "Behold, I am the handmaid of the Lord. May it be done to me according to your word" (Luke 1:38). It's about reflecting on how God's peace is most powerful when we're surrendering to His most unexpected plans.

Mary is no doubt the Queen, the prime model of faith and cooperation with grace. But she is that model, not simply because of who she is, but because of who God is and how she permitted Him to work in her life. The beautiful thing about Mary is that she didn't need to do anything but trust in God and act in faith in order to bring our Savior into the world. In the same way, we don't need to do anything wildly monumental when it comes to living out God's will in our lives; we simply need to trust that God will do the wildly monumental things in and through us and respond to His will through our words and deeds.

Further Reflection: Today, ask Mary to guide you closer to Jesus so that you might have a greater faith in Him. Pray a rosary, asking Mary to bring your intentions to Jesus.

SATURDAY OF THE FIRST WEEK OF ADVENT

Saturday, December 9th

Matthew 9:35–10:1, 5a, 6-8

Sometimes when I read the Gospels, I'm tempted to think of Jesus as some sort of untouchable, distant figure – like some person out of a history book or a statue in a museum – not a real, living, breathing, sensitive, feeling Person. But then, I'll read stories like today's Gospel where Matthew writes about how Jesus was affected by the crowds around Him, how "His heart was moved with pity for them because they were troubled and abandoned…" (Matthew 9). And I'll be reminded of just how real, approachable, and responsive He is – that He's not some cold, distant figure, but a real Person, that responds to me and my experiences.

This is the response that God has for us, and our sin. He is troubled by it. He has pity for our sad state. But He's not unmoved. He does something about it. He becomes man and saves us from it. God's heart is moved out of love for us, and by this love, we come to know the true peace we were created for – the true peace only known by living in relationship with Him.

As we close out this first week of Advent, I challenge you to take a moment to reflect, maybe journal, on the areas of your life that might be affecting God – that might be moving His heart with pity for you. Is it a relationship that's pulling you away from Him? Is it a habit that is slowly isolating you from real love? Is it an apathy that has caused you to settle for a life far less glorious than the one you were created for?

Whatever it may be, our God is affected by it and He doesn't want to abandon you in it – so much so that He became man so He could save you from it.

Further Reflection: As we get nearer to celebrating the wildly profound gift that is the Incarnation at Christmas, identify what areas of your life Jesus might look at with a heavy heart, what areas are robbing you of the peace He longs to give you, and give those parts of your life to Him. And then, when He comes in the power of profound peace, allow His grace to transform them into opportunities to know and love Him more.

EXPECTANT FAITH

The Second Week of Advent

December 10 - 16

Brittany Calavitta

THE SECOND SUNDAY OF ADVENT

Sunday, December 10th

Isaiah 40:1-5, 9-11
Psalm 85:9-14
2 Peter 3:8-14
Mark 1:1-8

Target is where self-control is put to the test. It is where a hefty appetite for happiness and fulfillment is subdued by cheap mascara and a cute pair of knock-off Keds. It is where I roam the aisles in search of bigger and greater. It is where the search for "something more" is pursued with vigor and determination.

And it's a dilemma, really, because just as the outside air brushes against the many shopping bags I clutch ever-so-tightly in my hands, I am filled with regret. I am filled with the what-ifs and could-haves from all of the merchandise I chose not to buy. Suddenly, that lime-green tank top pales in comparison to the burgundy pants I almost bought instead.

The search for happiness in this material world is common. We are continually told to do more, be more, have more, I feel it – that worldly pressure to measure up – in the perfectly tailored social media posts and the outrageous numbers found on designer price tags. So I run. I run to more and bigger and better. I run and run and run until my lungs are exhausted and my soul is disgusted.

There is a hunger inside of us all, and it outlasts whatever material goods we try to throw at it. It is an infinite void that we try to stuff with finite resources, assuming that happiness will follow the trail of material possessions, accomplishments, and accolades. So, we stuff and stuff and stuff with more and more and more. And that's where the fatigue will find you – sitting atop a pile of junk on a dry and deserted desert ground, thirsting for water.

And though this desert is the last place that we would choose to be, it is the very place where God begins to speak. Prompted by the Spirit, this Gospel greets us with John the Baptist crying out in into the wilderness, striking at the dusty ground in the desert of our hearts, beckoning us to "prepare the way of the Lord" (Mark 1:3).

But what does it mean to prepare? And why does it command us to cry fourth from a voice in the desert?

The word prepare comes from the Latin word "praeparare," which means to "make ready beforehand." It is a strong word, one of action and process. Behind the word, lies an abundance of expectation, and it is in that expectation that our willingness to practice the art of preparation can flourish. It is developed, for example, when we meet the expectation of a good grade by preparing in advance and studying for a test. It is put to good use when we meet the expectation of cheering crowds at the finish-line of a long race by preparing with practice beforehand. Expectation promotes preparation; the two go hand-in-hand.

It is the expectation of Christ's arrival that St. John the Baptist is awakening in today's reading. "One mightier than I is coming after me," he says in Mark 1:7. This is important because by awaking this expectation in their hearts, he is also implying preparation, for it was foretold in Isaiah, "Behold, I am sending my messenger ahead of you; he will prepare your way. A voice of one crying out in the desert: 'Prepare the way of the Lord, make straight his paths.'" (Mark 1:2-3).

We are called to the same sort of preparation. Amid the glow of twinkling lights and chestnuts roasting on the open fire, it is the celebration of Christ's arrival that beckons us to preparation, to quiet our hearts and make straight His path.

But, it's hard because at the very moment we are invited to quiet our hearts in hopeful expectation, we are also met with the clamor of chaos. The desert creeps back into our hearts masqueraded in tinsel and wrapping paper. It consumes us and leaves us without the very thing our souls yearn for – Christ.

There's something so poetic about St. John the Baptist's command coming forth from the desert, because it's so easy to get lost there around this time of year. It's easy to look to the gifts and the lights and the grandeur of the season, to try to fill and fill and fill the void in our souls with more and more and more. It is as if that familiar, deep void in us grows larger in December, and our deserted hearts ache with longing.

But it is in the parched soil that St. John the Baptist tells of "a baptism of repentance for the forgiveness of sins" (Mark 1:4). He enters the desolate land with a message of hope. That same hope is offered to us in our own desert – that void you try to fill with money and notoriety and additions. That hope is Christ. He is what your heart is seeking.

Come, let us prepare the way of the Lord.

Further Reflection: This week, ask yourself, what do I try to fill my life with? Material goods? Food? Affirmation? Fast from one of those items entirely this week.

MONDAY OF THE SECOND WEEK OF ADVENT

Monday, December 11ᵗʰ

Luke 5:17-26

There is currently a tiny army of bone spurs heading straight for my mother's spine. The doctors repeat words to her like, "paralysis" and "pain." Soon enough, she fears, she will lose all mobility in her neck as the spurs seek to fuse with her spine. And I see it – the way she winces when she shifts her head to the side, or the way she clutches the back of her neck in agony when the weather is particularly disagreeable.

"Pray," she says. So I do. I pray through fear and sympathy. But the whispers of fear are there. They deafen the faith in my heart and permeate my mind with doubt.

What do you do when the whispers surround, when their collective murmurs advance on your heart in loud and boisterous shouts of doubt? What do you do when your prayers become shrouded in skepticism and your confidence wanes in the face of the impossible? What do you do with a faith that is faithless?

I have to imagine that the men in today's Gospel heard those same whispers. I have to imagine they faced the same sort of human inclination to doubt. But it is their faith that speaks to my heart so profoundly because it is their faith that compelled them to scale a building in order to confront their paralyzed friend with the healing powers of Christ (Luke 5:19). These men were operating out of expectant faith. Amid whispers of doubt, they took bold steps in trust.

And sometimes, that's what our faith needs – action. We need faith like the men in today's Gospel, a faith that moves in the confidence of God's providence. So, when the whispers of doubt encircle your heart, act. Much like the men did in today's Gospel, confront your troubles with the very presence of Christ in the Eucharist. And while you sit in adoration with a heart full of fear, pray in expectant faith of a God who knows no bounds, and let Him fill your heart with grace.

Further Reflection: Respond to your doubt with action. Go to Adoration today or sometime this week. (If you don't have an Adoration chapel near you, find a church you can pray in.) In prayer, tell the Lord an area of trouble in your life and then ask for His guidance and peace.

FEAST OF OUR LADY OF GUADALUPE

Tuesday, December 12th

Luke 1:26-38 or 1:39-47

Nothing is impossible for God. It's a scary thought because the moment you fully allow yourself to become consumed by that belief is the very moment you allow yourself to become vulnerable. It's the moment your heart hinges on hope or fear or apprehension. It's the moment you realize that your control is lost in Him.

God was born of a virgin. God chose Mary to carry the Savior of the world. I can't imagine the fear that must have rattled through her bones. I can't imagine the tears that must have stained her cheeks or the questions that must have flooded her heart.

"For nothing will be impossible for God" (Luke 1:37).

We see the impossible made possible in today's reading. We see both the fear and the hope left in the wake of God's great plan, and it's easy to see how it plays out from over here, behind the pages of our Bibles. It's easy to see God's grace shine through the particular circumstances in this reading.

But it's not so easy in our own lives. Sometimes it's scary – the impossible He makes possible for us – because the impossible we want may not be the impossible He wants.

And it is there that we falter. It is there that we are overcome with worry trying to force the plans we have set for our lives. But it's only in God's design for us that true peace is found. So, let us live in the expectant faith that God will provide, even when it seems scary.

Further Reflection: Bring your seemingly impossible circumstances to the very place the impossible is found – Mass. When your heart is fraught with fear, kneel before Christ on the altar and whisper the words of Mary in today's Gospel, "May it be done to me according to your word" (Luke 1:38).

MEMORIAL OF ST. LUCY, VIRGIN AND MARTYR

Wednesday, December 13th

———————

Matthew 11:28-30

———————

As I am writing this, my heart is heavy. It is heavy from weeks of stress and illness and exhaustion. My son sleeps in the next room with a number on the thermometer that sent us straight to Urgent Care this afternoon. A notice about a rent increase sits on our counter and has me frantically trying to find an affordable place to move. And on top of it all, ants have infiltrated our apartment in the hopes of expediting our moving process.

My home and heart are in disorder.

You know what I'm talking about, don't you? Haven't you been here before? You felt the sting of the massive "F" slapped across the front of that important test you spent hours studying for. Your heart grew distressed by the words your mother's doctor shared with her the day you found out she was sick. You felt dejection when your excited eyes couldn't understand why you saw such a negative response in a text message.

Sometimes it feels hard to breathe, doesn't it? Like the weight of the world is pressing in, causing you to panic.

In Matthew 11:28, Jesus says, "Come to me, all you who labor and are burdened, and I will give you rest."

Do you trust Him? Do you live your life with faith that God will find rest for your troubled soul?

On those days when the sun is shining and your heart is happy, it's easy to trust in His words. It's easy to lift your hands in praise to a God who provides. But it's the hard days that matter. It's the hard days that make us doubt. It's the hard days that replace our faith with worry. But, those are also the days that God invites us to join Him in peace. He tells us in Matthew 11:30 that "[His] yoke is easy, and [His] burden is light."

So, trust Him. When your heart is heavy with worry or failure or dejection, take it to Him in prayer, praise Him for the peace He provides, and trust that He is who He says He is. He will give you rest.

Further Reflection: In prayer today, pray this simple prayer: "God, you are good." Pray this prayer until you believe it.

MEMORIAL OF ST. JOHN OF THE CROSS, PRIEST AND DOCTOR OF THE CHURCH

Thursday, December 14th

Matthew 11:11-15

The road between heaven and hell is fraught with warfare. It is an arduous journey full of temptation, sin, and glorious grace.

Sometimes I think we forget that. I see it in the way we mosey up to the front of the altar for communion, our hands folded out of habit as a lackluster, "Amen," escapes our lips. Complacency has penetrated our souls. It has taken our churches hostage and enraptured us with the illusion of safety as it casts its false shadow on our faith. But we should not be complacent in faith: our faith is a battle. It is a skirmish with hell over the salvation of our very souls. Jesus reminds us of this in Matthew 11:12 when He says, "the violent are taking [heaven] by force."

Are you part of the fight? Is your heart worn from prayer? Are your feet blistered from service?

We often live as though our faith is fragile, that it is only something to reveal in churches or hide away behind silent prayers. Our understanding of what Catholicism really is has been altered by the promise of a neatly packaged version of Christianity. But faith is messy. It is complicated and raw and beautiful.

Let's proceed with this expectation of faith, this version of Christianity that sets our hearts ablaze in fiery warfare. Let us love ferociously in a world of hate and pray unceasingly for the hearts that need it. And as we wait in joyful expectation for the coming of Christ, may we ready our hearts for the battlefield. May we ready our hearts for heaven.

Further Reflection: Today, take some time to journal about the ways that you have fought for your faith. If you have trouble coming up with a response to this prompt, consider why that is and journal about it.

FRIDAY OF THE SECOND WEEK OF ADVENT

Friday, December 15th

Matthew 11:16-19

I saw the spots on her the first day I met her. They were impossible to hide. They plastered her skin with splotchy pigmentation and marked her as different. But it wasn't the difference in her skin that I noticed as much as the difference in her demeanor. Because each time my eyes met hers with a welcoming grin, her eyes met mine with a pessimistic scowl.

And that was it. That was enough for me to deem her as "unfriendly." That was enough to halt my welcomes and close my heart.

Her mom came into our class one warm, April day. She explained to us her daughter's condition and told the story of a hurting soul behind splotchy skin. She told of a heart with wounds and a body wrecked by tumors. She shared of a love that faltered under the shame and embarrassment of her illness.

That's when my heart shifted. That's the day I decided to make her my best friend. Twenty-one years have passed since that day. Twenty-one years of laughter and friendship and love that I almost let slip by because of assumed expectations I placed on her.

I see those expectations so prevalently in today's reading. "For John came neither eating nor drinking, and they said, 'He is possessed by a demon.' The Son of Man came eating and drinking and they said, 'Look, he is a glutton and a drunkard, a friend of tax collectors and sinners'" (Matthew 11:18-19).

It's easy to make assumptions from the outside, looking in – to see John as a demon, or Jesus as a drunkard. But there is so much more to see if you'd allow it, if you'd recognize that it's on the inside that the truest parts of us shine.

Seek it out. Live in expectant faith full of open mindedness, love, and forgiveness. Look for the light in others, even when darkness surrounds, for there is good to be found on the inside.

Further Reflection: Is there someone in your life you have struggled to see the light of Christ within? Today, pray for that person and ask the Lord to help you to see His light within him or her.

SATURDAY OF THE SECOND WEEK OF ADVENT

Saturday, December 16ᵗʰ

———————

Matthew 17:9a, 10-13

———————

I always worry that I won't live up to expectations. I worry that my efforts will fall short in the clamor and chaos of daily life, that my time won't possibly stretch enough to properly meet the needs of the deadlines and appointments and notifications that continually flood my frazzled mind.

Today's reading has me thinking a lot about expectations. When asked of Elijah's coming, Jesus responds to His disciples by saying, "Elijah will indeed come and restore all things; but I tell you that Elijah has already come, and they did not recognize him but did to him whatever they pleased" (Matthew 17:11-12).

They did not recognize Him. Why? Did they expect something different?

And here we find ourselves, in a season of expectation. We wait for Him – a baby born of a virgin. Isn't that interesting? The God of the universe came as a tiny, helpless baby. Do we see power and strength and salvation in someone so small?

God comes to us in unexpected ways. He captures our hearts with bread and wine, and saves our souls with blood and wood.

We get so caught up in earthly expectations that sometimes we miss the heavenly ones – those grace-filled moments God sneaks into the fabric of life.

So, the next time you feel it – that stress-filled need to meet those earthly expectations, stop. Quiet your heart in humble surrender and remember that there is a God who is bigger and greater and stronger. He is waiting to flood your heart with heavenly expectation. You just have to let Him.

Further Reflection: What are you stressed out about today? Take a moment to reflect on this. Then, ask the Lord to help you recognize where He is within that stress. If needed, pray this prayer: "God, you are bigger than (name the specific situation that is causing stress)." Repeat this prayer until God's grace overwhelms you with peace.

JOYFUL HUMILITY

The Third Week of Advent

December 17 - 23

―――――――――

Joel Stepanek

THE THIRD SUNDAY OF ADVENT

Sunday, December 17ᵗʰ

Isaiah 61:1-2a, 10-11
Luke 1:46-48, 49-50, 53-54
1 Thessalonians 5:16-24
John 1:6-8, 19-28

It is hard for me to not be the best. I don't like losing – I never have. When I was younger, I used to have a terrible temper and would stay mad for hours if I lost a game. I want to be number one. And really, who doesn't? It feels good to win, to be on top, to be admired and successful. For a long time, I thought that success was the key to joy. I would say, "If I can just achieve this one thing, I will know true joy. I'll be happy."

I got into the school I wanted to get into for college.

I got really good grades and was popular. I was the class speaker at my college commencement.

I got the job I wanted to get.

I was affirmed, applauded, and sometimes considered, "the best." I thought I would be joyful – but that feeling left almost as soon as I found it, and I couldn't shake the feeling of emptiness.

This kind of joy – the joy that comes from success – is really false joy. I have moments where I rejoice, but they are fleeting and I am left empty. Without fail, once I get what I want, it suddenly doesn't matter anymore. Maybe I'll be happy for a little bit, but the feeling fades. After the victory, I immediately look for the next. It takes a lot of work to be the best, to stay on top. And it brings a lot of anxiety. If my identity is only found in being the greatest, what happens when I'm not?

Today's readings taught me something, a lesson that is hard to hear and apply but brings amazing freedom. *The path to true joy lies in humility.*

When I was a kid, I always noticed that the color for this Sunday of Advent changed to pink (or, as any priest will correct you, "rose"). We call it "Gaudete Sunday," or "Joyful Sunday." The word "rejoice" is present in the first three readings.

That word challenges me with a question, "Where do I find my joy?" Do I find it in moments or people or in something greater? Do I find it in things that will ultimately let me down and leave me wanting more or in something that can really satisfy me?

This is where I need to learn humility. When I try to put myself above God, it doesn't work – I can't control the universe and I wind up unhappy. But if I submit to God, then I find freedom in recognizing that my God is trustworthy and His promises are true. He knows what is best for me and wants to give me what I need.

I've realized that humility requires something, though. It requires prayer; the kind of prayer that continually says, "thy will be done" to God, who is greater than my hopes and longings. This is how we pray unceasingly. I've realized that it is why humility, prayer, and joy go together. It is why, as a community, we pause on the Third Sunday in Advent to rejoice – God is coming to meet us. Just like that pink shocked me out of my routine as a kid, it wakes me from my Advent sleep as an adult. God is coming to save me.

Joy is found in this realization, and sustainable joy is found in humbly serving the God that meets us and gives us life. It is found in being close to the shoelaces of a God that keeps our lives tied together, undoing knots and making us more than we could ever be if left on our own.

Further Reflection: Find a way to humble yourself today and serve someone else; if possible, do it in such a way that they don't know you served. Then, offer up prayers for the soul of that person.

MONDAY OF THE THIRD WEEK OF ADVENT

Monday, December 18th

Matthew 1:18-25

I hate watching the news. Every time I see an article online, video, or something someone shares I think the same thing: Things are not as they should be in our world.

I see people hurt each other in serious and lasting ways. I watch nations threaten each other with war and send machines into battle with the intent of destroying one another. Loved ones die from disease and accidents. It breaks my heart. I think about how this week started with readings about "rejoicing always" and how we find joy in the Lord, but on Monday morning

I find my "Joyful Sunday" sobered by the images on my screen.

How can we find joy in a world so broken? My life can be so messy. Where is God in that?

God brings justice. I used to think of justice as a midday courtroom show or a way we determine right and wrong. But, I've realized it is really about "right relationships." The readings today give me hope in God's restorative justice. There is a prophetic voice telling the people that one day exile will end and Israel will be restored. There will be freedom. In the Psalm, God's justice is praised – not because He stands with a gavel waiting to sentence people to hell – but because when we live in the justice of God, we live in harmony with Him and each other. All is right. Advent remembers the birth of Christ, but also looks ahead to the Final Judgment – the time when God will make all things new and restore broken hearts.

The mess isn't forever. There is hope on Monday morning.

Above all, I look at what God can do with a betrothed couple whose world became messy. Mary and Joseph's lives were turned upside down, but God had plans that were deeper than they could ever realize. Jesus was with them (literally) in the mess. And Jesus is with me in mine. He is with you in yours. God doesn't look dispassionately upon our mess and the difficult realities of our lives. Instead, He enters into them. That is cause for me to rejoice, even in my mess – because it is out of that mess that my God finds me and makes all things new.

Further Reflection: We often keep our mess a secret. Invite God, through prayer, into a mess that exists in your life. If your "mess" is a relationship, take one step today toward restoring that relationship, even if it is just praying for the good of the other person.

TUESDAY OF THE THIRD WEEK OF ADVENT

Tuesday, December 19ᵗʰ

Luke 1:5-25

There are things I don't think God can fix. I'm not talking about the challenges that the world faces that sometimes rob me of my joy on Monday morning. I'm talking about areas of my life where I feel like God has just given up or forgotten me.

A few years ago, I went on a silent retreat. On one of the final days I listed a bunch of things that I felt were "impossible" for God and essentially said, "Lord, I trust you with these areas of my life – even though I feel like they are impossible and you've forgotten me, I trust you. I praise you, even when you seem distant." With that simple, honest prayer, my heart experienced healing in the weeks and months after that retreat. I am reminded of this prayer when I read today's readings. I am reminded that God's glory is revealed in the impossible, and it is praise that reminds us that His glory is indeed possible.

Today's readings talk about two women who live with a broken, seemingly impossible reality: they can't bear children. For a Jewish woman, that was almost shameful. The perception was that God was displeased with them, perhaps had even abandoned them. If children were a blessing from God, what does that mean for a woman who can't give birth?

I am sure both women in the readings today (Samson's mother and Elizabeth) had times they doubted God, maybe even were angry with God. Have you ever felt that sting of "abandonment?" It happens in the dark moments when our prayers seemingly go unheard and God appears to be unresponsive. Too often we mistake God's silence as disapproval or even rejection. What should our response be in those moments when we feel rejected?

Praise.

God has not abandoned you. God moves in silence. God has more in store for you than you would plan for yourself. While you wait, embrace praise. God's glory is revealed in our "impossible."

Further Reflection: If you are dealing with an impossible situation, feel like God has forgotten you, or are just struggling in this Advent season, write a prayer of praise to God. Pray it every day through the rest of this season.

WEDNESDAY OF THE THIRD WEEK OF ADVENT

Wednesday, December 20th

———————

Luke 1:26-38

———————

I don't like it when people try to pay for my meal. But I also really like it when people pay for my meal. It is both insulting and flattering. On the one hand, I don't want that person to pay for my meal and I feel like I should fight them on it:

"No, no, don't do that. I can pay for my own."

But deep down, I am flattered someone is paying for me. I am honored they want to gift me that meal and (partially) happy I don't have to spend my own money. A friend's mom once taught me a valuable lesson in high school when I tried to fight her on a bill, "Don't fight my kindness. Just say, 'thank you.'"

In the First Reading, King Ahaz gets a once in a lifetime offer. The prophet Isaiah tells him that God will provide a sign of His presence – all Ahaz needs to do is ask. Ahaz thinks he knows the right answer: He protests. "I will not tempt the Lord by asking for a sign."

At first, Isaiah's response to him seems harsh. Isn't Ahaz just trying to be humble? Ahaz is actually just the opposite – false humility is really pride. He is trying to look the part of being faithful, but is actually a bad king. His response isn't genuine.

God continually offers me incredible things, and I am continually astounded at how often I reject them. I miss the blessing because it isn't what I expect or what I am looking for or, maybe to keep myself safe, I don't ask God for big things. I don't bring my big prayers to Him and I justify it by saying, "God has other things to worry about. I'm not worth the time."

My response (and yours) to God's generosity needs to mirror Mary, the "sign" that Ahaz refused, in accepting with humility what God offers. Mary doesn't fight the angel. She doesn't fight the Lord. She doesn't protest or say, "What happens next?" She is grateful to be chosen by God and rejoices in humility. God does great things for her because she was open. God will do the same for us today – all we need to do is stop protesting.

Sometimes humility is accepting that someone else is going to pay; after all, that is the cross. Sometimes humility is simply saying, "thank you" to the gift someone gives rather than trying to justify why we don't deserve it. We don't deserve the manger. We don't deserve the cross. Yet God, in His love and providence, offers it anyway, freely. Receive that gift, freely, today.

Further Reflection: Let someone do something good for you today.

THURSDAY OF THE THIRD WEEK OF ADVENT

Thursday, December 21st

Luke 1:39-45

I can handle being thankful for the blessings that God gives me. The real struggle is being thankful when someone close to me is blessed and I (in my sinful perception) believe that I am not. Too often, rather than being happy for that person, I get jealous. I even get mad. Today's Gospel hits me in the face with a simple message:

Love rejoices.

It just can't contain itself. It needs to celebrate the victories and accomplishments of those that we love. It rejoices in the good things God does, whether they impact us or not. In the Gospel, Mary sets out "in haste" to meet Elizabeth. She is going to celebrate. Elizabeth finally is going to have a child after years of being barren.

Mary isn't there to talk about her own big news.

It is much easier to talk about our own victories than it is to talk about the victories of our friends. We get jealous more easily and even try to "one up" one another. Do you know someone like that? No matter what you share, no matter how good the news is, they always have something better to say. The "one up" mentality comes from our insecurity and pride. We don't want the spotlight taken off us, so instead, we find a way to make someone else's life and accomplishments seem less than our own. It is easier to celebrate ourselves than it is to be a supporting cast celebrating another person's leading role. The person I know like that is me. I can be terribly prideful and jealous.

But Mary, humble and joyful, goes quickly to Elizabeth to celebrate. Her heart convicts me. Mary is carrying the Savior of the world in her womb, yet her love for her cousin causes her to rejoice in Elizabeth's good news. If we could emulate Mary in anticipating each other's joys, in caring more about honoring them before ourselves, the dynamics of our community would change. It must begin somewhere, though – and today it can begin with us. Love rejoices with those whom we love.

Further Reflection: Celebrate a friend's accomplishments today.

FRIDAY OF THE THIRD WEEK OF ADVENT

Friday, December 22ⁿᵈ

Luke 1:46-56

Imagine: A friend shows up to your house with a gift. You open it up and realize it is something you've wanted for a long time. What is your next move? Of course, you thank that person – maybe even hug them or cry a little – and then you enjoy your gift. It would seem crazy to thank the person wholeheartedly for the gift and then give it back.

The First Reading today should shock us because that is exactly what happens. Several times, just this week alone, we've read about women that were barren and could have no children, but God gave them that gift. Today, Hannah presents her child,

Samuel, to the Lord (as is customary). In this ritual, parents of their firstborn son present him back to God as a gift. They recognize that every good thing comes from God; then, as part of the ritual they "ransom" the child back with an animal sacrifice. In this case, though, Hannah leaves her son with the temple priest. She gives him back completely to God. Why?

Because knowing God provides is enough. Knowing God heard her prayer was enough. She so radically trusted God that she knew God would take care of her son in the temple. And God does, Samuel is the prophet that anoints David as king, and it is through the line of David that Jesus is born. The child was only part of the gift; knowing that God hears and provides is the rest of it.

This is the question I hear from God daily, and I often struggle to respond:

Is My providence enough for you? Is the reality that I love you and care for you enough?

I am usually looking for bigger gifts – if such things could exist – to satisfy me. Everything I have is a gift from God; but I struggle to offer it back with the prayer, "Lord, your love is enough for me."

I would be so free if I could do that daily – just offer up this simple prayer found in the Gospel – Mary rejoicing in the God that has done great things for her. I want my response to God's good gifts to echo her praise.

Further Reflection: Take time to write out the good gifts God has given you. Try to think of things you often forget. Then, spend time in prayer thanking God for these gifts.

SATURDAY OF THE THIRD WEEK OF ADVENT

Saturday, December 23rd

Luke 1:57-66

"Rejoice – God has great plans for you."

Some days, it is harder for me to read that statement than others. Some days, that statement inspires me and gives me incredible consolation and hope. This week we encountered countless people that reacted both negatively and positively to that statement – just like you and me. And in all cases, one truth resounds: God provides for us, we simply need to encounter this truth and trust in Him. God's promises are secure.

God had great plans for John the Baptist – the First Reading tells about his coming.

What God speaks about John is also true for us. We've experienced Christ. We know Him. We become the messenger of this great news; this is the plan God has for us. Our entire lives are made to glorify Christ.

And in that glorification, we find joy. We humbly acknowledge that God is God and we are not; we recognize that we need a savior and are freed. We become free from the expectation to have it all together. We become liberated from the idea that our lives have no meaning or worth. We become free to share the Gospel and invite others into a relationship with our Lord.

In the coming days, many gifts will be exchanged. How do we share the gift of Christ with others? How will we lead others to that manger and to that cross? We are the messengers of God's salvation – in humility and joy we go forward to share it.

Further Reflection: Put a post-it note of the phrase, "God has great plans for you" on your mirror. Look at it every day and pray, "thy will be done" as a prayer of openness to the incredible things God has planned for you that day.

CALLED BY CHRIST

The Octave of Christmas

December 24 - January 1

Rachel Peñate

THE FOURTH SUNDAY OF ADVENT

Sunday, December 24th

---

2 Samuel 7:1-5, 8b-12, 14a, 16
Psalm 89:2-3, 4-5, 27, 29
Romans 16:25-27
Luke 1:26-38

Growing up, I was not what you call an athletic kid. I usually got picked last for teams in gym class and failed (somewhat) miserably at every sport I tried. But, it didn't phase me much as I grew awkwardly into my body; any time I "failed," I would just retreat to the activities that I was good at. Ultimately, I really didn't care that I wasn't good at sports.

But, for some reason (still unknown to me today), in the spring of my eighth grade year that all changed. That was the year

I was determined to run the entirety of our school mile. So, I trained. Well, I ran around the block a few times, gradually increasing my distance foot by foot. I worked to increase my endurance, and you better believe I ran that entire mile without stopping.

Something sparked in me that year I turned 14, a call within to do something I never thought I could accomplish. I realized with one simple decision that I was far more capable that I thought – I just needed to do something about it. What started as a mysterious inkling to complete a stubborn challenge has turned into a lifelong passion for running. Who knew the clumsy girl who preferred a book over the monkey bars would come to love running half-marathons?

God sure did.

God has given us the courage to accept the challenge and begin the race, to recognize that we are called to greatness. He calls us to truly believe that we are able to accomplish the plan He has for us – a plan that is greater than our doubt and fear.

I imagine Mary recognized this same call when she was visited by the Angel Gabriel – she saw deep within herself that she was capable of all it would take to say, "yes" to God's will for her life. And so, she stepped out in faith, trusting in the Lord.

"Behold, I am the Handmaid of the Lord" (Luke 1:38).

By calling herself "handmaid," she recognized her unique role in the salvation of the world. She was unafraid, responding with confidence, because she knew Who was calling her to this task.

What Mary recognized in God's call (through His messenger, Gabriel) was three-fold:

1. **God was calling her to respond.** And she did. "May it be done unto me according to your word" (Luke 1:38). May it be done. God called, and Mary answered.
2. **He had great things in store for her.** The mother of the "Son of the Most High." Whew. Yeah, that's a high calling.
3. **God would be with her.** "Hail Full of Grace, the Lord is with you... you have found favor with God" (Luke 1:28). God was with her; He would give her the grace she needed.

These are the same three things God is calling us to recognize with each and every task He places upon our hearts.

I am so grateful for Mary's witness. Who better than this quiet, trusting woman to teach us that *boldness in faith doesn't have to be dramatic or complicated.* As Mary's "yes" to God was specific to God's will for her life – your countless "yeses" will look different, each one lining the route of your own unique story.

The season of Advent ends tomorrow, but your journey with Christ is far from over. My prayer for you is that this season has been one of hope, joy, and renewal; that this season has been one of recognition that Christ is forever next to you on your journey.

His call requires your response. These next nine days are yours to discover the answer to one simple question:

How will you respond?

Further Reflection: Consider today your answers to the following questions and, if needed, journal about them. Where is God calling you today that requires your "yes"? Do you believe He has great things in store for you? Do you believe He is with you always?

NATIVITY OF THE LORD

Monday, December 25th

Isaiah 52:7-10
Psalm 98:1, 2-3, 3-4, 5-6
Hebrews 1:1-6
John 1:1-18

When was the last time you truly believed what you heard? I'm talking the sure-footed, unmoving certainty that what you are hearing with your ears is true, absolutely true?

God became man.

Did you feel that in your core?

What would our lives look like if we truly believed that reality? What would our hearts look like if we fully recognized the love that entered our world when the

Word became Flesh?

Today, we remember when Christ entered the world.

I'm not talking about the entrance you would make into a party, or the kind where you come riding in on a white horse. I'm talking about the messy, humble, breathtaking entrance of a baby – the type of entrance that would leave anyone pondering the miracle of existence.

Christ chose, thousands of years ago, that it wasn't enough to just "show up" and heal our wounds. No. He opted to take our wounds upon Himself. He became man – He took on humanity in its fullness, like us in all things but sin – so that He could show us just how big His love is.

This is what we celebrate today.

In the mess of wrapping paper and gifts, give glory to God for taking on flesh. In the melodies of Christmas carols, give glory to God for sending down His Word. In the quiet moments by the fire, give glory to God for His sacrifice.

He gave so that we could receive. What a truly incredible Savior.

Further Reflection: Spend intentional time with your family today – be present to them. And in everything, give all glory to God.

FEAST OF ST. STEPHEN, FIRST MARTYR

Tuesday, December 26ᵗʰ

Matthew 10:17-22

I am as Type-A as you can get. I color coordinate my books and alphabetize my movies. Put something in a place it doesn't belong, and I'll follow you around to tell you where it actually goes. My planner may as well be my life, and it's surprising that my desire to keep everything neat and tidy hasn't put me in an early grave.

Some days, I feel like I need total control of my surroundings to survive. Those are usually the days that God reminds me I don't. If there is anything that He has taught me, it's that He calls us to respond to Him even in the messiest moments of life.

God called St. Stephen in a moment of chaos. Saint Stephen responded with everything. He responded with his entire life.

In today's Gospel, Jesus speaks words of wisdom that beat at the heart of St. Stephen's actions. "When they hand you over, do not worry about how you are to speak or what you are to say. You will be given at that moment what you are to say" (Matthew 10:19). In that moment of utter loss, St. Stephen could've complained for what wasn't his to control. He could've thrown his fist up at God (or thrown a temper tantrum, as I probably would have done) and whined about the fact that God didn't immediately clean up the situation. Instead, St. Stephen allowed the Holy Spirit to work through him right in that precarious moment, to be his voice – a voice of reason and love.

God still has a plan, even when you are in the midst of unknown, chaotic moments. When the plan you had set out for yourself all of a sudden looks very different. When the house is a mess, and that to-do list is still sitting untouched. When you realize you may have said something hurtful and your heart is beating rapidly in fear, worried you messed it all up. When your head is just simply spinning.

God *still* has a plan.

Breathe in that truth, and find peace and joy knowing that He is in control.

Further Reflection: What keeps you from opening your hands and letting go of what you're clinging to? In a moment of prayer, close your eyes and open your hands. Bring to mind what "mess" is in your life that you want control over. Think on it for a few minutes and then ask God to take it from you. Ask Him to fill you with the confidence to know that He truly is in control. Consider today that God is calling you to allow Him to enter into the mess of your life. Will you let Him?

FEAST OF ST. JOHN, APOSTLE AND EVANGELIST

Wednesday, December 27th

John 20:1a, 2-8

I knew a girl in college who could make everyone smile whenever they were around her. She always carried with her a look of intense joy that emanated from within. I'll admit, sometimes it drove me crazy – who could really be that happy? Who could really be that excited about life? The more I got to know her though, the more I realized her joy was genuine; it was something to be admired. She loved life because she loved the Creator of life.

Today's Gospel kicks me in the pants. When have I been so excited that I've literally raced someone else to see if this cause for joy was really true? Probably not since I was five...

Today, we reflect on the miracle of Easter because this is the reason for Christmas. Christ didn't just enter this world to hang out with us. He had a mission, and He did not leave us until that mission was accomplished. When we remember and celebrate the life of Christ, let us also celebrate the death of Christ, because without His death, we would not have life.

We would not have life.

Jesus' rising from the dead was a big deal. Jesus died and rose so that we could be redeemed! He gave His life freely so that we could (undeservedly) have the merit of heaven. It makes sense that Mary and the apostles' ran to the tomb, overcome with joy. What do we do when we hear – or rehear – this good news? Do we rejoice? Do we let it transform our entire life?

Further Reflection: Today, Christ calls us to zealous love – to a life of jubilant thanksgiving. Who is a person in your life that exudes joy? Or, who is a person who needs to hear the merciful Word of God? Like Mary did with the apostles, seek that person out today, and share the everlasting love of Christ with him or her.

FEAST OF THE HOLY INNOCENTS, MARTYRS

Thursday, December 28th

Matthew 2:13-18

When we were little, my brother and I were terrified of the dark hallway leading to our bedrooms. Like the deep end of the pool, the hallway always seemed much longer and scarier when we couldn't see to the end. But, it was amazing how quickly that fear transpired into confidence when we sucked it up and ran to the light switch at the end of the hallway, knowing the flick of the tiny switch would dissipate our fear.

Light changes things. What was once unknown became known. What was once long and daunting became short and easy. Just like that switch, Christ changes things.

Today's Gospel is hard to digest. As a new mom, I think about my darkest fear, of losing my sweet baby, and this Gospel brings me to my knees. But, the thing about fear is that when we place it in the light, the lie of darkness starts to be revealed. In our greatest fears, Christ's light brings truth; and, truth brings peace.

Today's feast of the Holy Innocents – the remembrance of King Herod's massacre of infants in attempt to kill Jesus – reminds us that as long as there is sin is in the world, there will be darkness. Anger will cause division, pride will eliminate humility, and selfishness will destroy life. But, "if we walk in the light as He is in the light, then we have fellowship with one another, and the blood of his Son Jesus cleanses us from all sin" (1 John 1:7).

We are called to the light of Christ.

If only we run to Him, He will be the brilliant light that illuminates our darkness. We need only to seek Him when we are unable to see the way, to turn to Him when we need confidence and strength.

Further Reflection: Where do you encounter darkness in your life? Have you invited the Light of the World into it? When all seems lost, remember: the greater the darkness, the more brilliant the light (John 1:5). Do not fear where He is calling you. Go, for He is with you.

THE FIFTH DAY IN THE OCTAVE OF CHRISTMAS

Friday, December 29ᵗʰ

Luke 2:22-35

Recently, I was involved in an interview process. My co-workers and I prepared questions ahead of time and there was one question in particular that, every time we asked it, I wondered how I would respond: "What types of people bother you?"

I'm sure I'd think it was a trick question, or at least be hesitant to answer. But, I'd be lying if I didn't say I knew exactly how I would reply: people who don't follow through on their promises.

It's easy to talk a "big talk," to make promises, to tell someone what you'd like your expected outcome to be:

"Yeah, I'm going study diligently for my tests."

"I can totally pick you up at seven! No, I won't be late."

"I won't tell anyone your secret."

"I won't take advantage of you."

It's easy, because the old adage is true: "talk is cheap." We can talk and talk and talk, but until we act, our words are worthless.

"Whoever says, 'I know him,' but does not keep his commandments is a liar" (1 John 2:4).

This line from 1 John makes me shake in my boots. I say I know God all the time – in my conversations with friends, on social media, and with strangers. But, do I act in a way that shows that I know God? Do I speak about my friends in a way that would honor them as God's good creation? Do I show up to church on Sunday and pray? Do I dress and talk in such a way that shows I know my own dignity and worth?

If I really knew God, I'd know that He calls me to live authentically – to live according to His virtues and commandments.

For every promise we make, there is a virtue that can help us follow through on that commitment. God never breaks His promises to us. Let us learn from Him and lean on Him when we need a little bit of encouragement.

Further Reflection: Think back to Sunday and recall the promises you made this week. Have you followed through on all of them? If not, which one(s) can you follow through on today?

THE SIXTH DAY IN THE OCTAVE OF CHRISTMAS

Saturday, December 30th

Luke 2:36-40

Spend a significant amount of time with any three-year-old and you probably will find yourself exhausted. Those little human beings are a tornado of questions. Why is the sun bright? Why do cars drive? What is the color of the air? Why does my hair grow? Why this? Why that? Why? Why? Why?

So often, I approach prayer like a three-year-old. *Why are you calling me to this plan Lord? (Two seconds later:) What did you say? I can't hear you, ugh, I guess I need to make it up.* I flood God with questions, but am annoyed when I am left with more questions than answers. But, what I miss with this mentality is exactly what those little three year olds are lacking: patience.

God will always answer our questions - it just may not be in the manner or timing we would like.

In today's Gospel, Anna demonstrates an awe-inspiring amount of patience. If you look at this reading closely, you'll notice that she remained in the temple for decades after her husband died. Decades! She persisted in prayer and she remained faithful to the Lord – "worshipp[ing] night and day." Anna desired answers, so she waited. She waited and waited, persisting in prayer while allowing God to respond in His perfect timing.

God may not be calling us to this same type of fervent prayer, but He does call us to be insistent and patient in our prayer. As a little kid insists on knowing the answer for the sake of better understanding the world, we too should insist on knowing the answer for the sake of better understanding the answer giver. We are called to be insistent in our prayer because *a relationship with God is not just a series of fleeting moments but a lifetime of intimate conversation.* God desires to reveal Himself and His plan to us. May we have the patience to allow Him to answer in His perfect way and timing.

Further Reflection: What is one specific question you've been waiting for the Lord to answer? Take that question to Him again today, but don't seek the answer – seek the peace in knowing He hears your prayer.

THE HOLY FAMILY OF JESUS, MARY, AND JOSEPH

Sunday, December 31ˢᵗ

Sirach 3:2-6, 12-14
Psalm 128:1-2, 3, 4-5
Colossians 3:12-21
Luke 2:22-40

I still remember that day. I remember the nonchalant nature of the conversation, yet weight of his words. "You do know, Rachel, I wouldn't still be Catholic if it weren't for you." I would've easily missed the profundity of my brother's statement if it weren't for the fact that his affirmation was a 20-year answer to a deep prayer.

In every moment since I first learned who Christ was, my one desire was to take my family on the journey with me. But, it is hard. Oh, so hard. (I'm sure many of you are nodding in empathy.)

Those closest to us are often the hardest to talk to about the matters that are nearest to our hearts. Because, when they reject those matters, it feels like they are rejecting our hearts. I've encountered countless occasions of heartache when it comes to my family. In these moments of heartache, I thought I was failing them; God made it clear otherwise. You see, God had taught me that my family's salvation wasn't my doing, but His. There was nothing special that I did to encourage my brother to recognize and accept the faith, but it was in my genuine pursuit of God that he was inspired to genuinely pursue God as well.

God did all the work; all I needed to do was authentically respond to His love.

Do you ever experience moments where you get caught up in the lie that you need to be someone else's savior? That for some reason you think your words or prayers are going to earn them salvation?

Some days, I still struggle with putting this pressure on my shoulders. Some days, I recognize that pride is what's causing me to believe this lie that I can earn them salvation; other days, it's downright stubbornness and determination to get a certain family member to heaven. It's important to pray for and never give up on our loved ones. But, the First Reading from Sirach teaches us today that seeking a family member's holiness is all about authentic love. Speak when you need to, serve in the way you need to serve, and then let God take care of the rest.

Further Reflection: How can you love your family well today? Pray for them? Do an act of service for them? Or, simply, be with them with no other intention than to spend time with them? Whatever you do, offer your family members back to the Lord and ask Him to give you the grace and peace needed to know that He is taking care of their every need.

SOLEMNITY OF THE BLESSED VIRGIN MARY, THE MOTHER OF GOD

Monday, January 1st

Luke 2:16-21

HAAAAAPY NEW YEAR!! Cue fireworks and kazoos, balloon drops and glitter confetti, yelling from rooftops and powerful ballads promising this to be the best year yet!

Okay... that may not be the sentiment for everyone today. You may have had a spectacular celebration to ring in the new year and have high hopes for your New Year's resolutions. But, maybe, you struggled to stay awake long enough to see the Times Square Ball Drop. Maybe you forgot about it entirely and, surprise – it's January 1st.

We're all on different roads to begin this new year. But, regardless of what your road ahead looks like, we're here, contemplating the Gospel for this awesome day: The Solemnity of the Blessed Virgin Mary, the Mother of God (just breathe in that title for a moment). So, rejoice! God has given you a mother, the Mother of God, who teaches us what it means to live an invigorating life in Christ; who teaches us how to begin a new year in Him.

So, you may ask, what is Mary's secret to a life in Christ? It's simple. Acknowledge what He has done for you, and be grateful.

The shepherds in our Gospel today are the first to exemplify what it means to acknowledge the Lord's plans and rejoice. When they heard the message that a Savior had been born in the city of David (Luke 2:10-11), they dropped everything and went to that city, hoping this prophecy was true. And when they arrived in Bethlehem, their hope was realized – they saw Jesus, "the infant lying in the manger" and "made known the message" to all that were present, including Our Lady.

While the shepherds and all others who heard this message reacted outwardly – "glorifying and praising God" – Mary's reaction was different. Mary "kept all these things, pondering on them in her heart." Why would she do that? She didn't yell from the rooftops or hide from this powerful proclamation; she reflected and kept this news in her heart.

We too encounter moments like Mary and the shepherds, in which the Lord answers a specific prayer, breathes truth into our lives, or calls us to a path that is beautiful and a little scary. We might react outwardly with joy or hide in fear. These are authentic reactions, but we learn from Mary that reflection is important.

We can only imagine Mary's reflection on God's promise that He would send a savior is what kept her so calm throughout Jesus' ministry, and ultimately His death on the cross. For even though it was painful to watch her Son give His life in such a gruesome way, we can imagine it was the knowledge of and faith in what God had already done in her life that was a constant reminder to trust His plan. Reflection requires us to dig deep into the mystery of God, and in turn we discover so much more about Him and the beautiful ways He is working in our lives.

Closing Reflection: As we close this retreat, bring to mind all that God has taught you this Advent and Christmas Octave. Take some time and write it down. Then, pause and pray, ask God what He is calling you to beyond this season. Ask Him to reveal to you – if even just a snippet – of the plans He has for you.

Recognize all that He has done for you, but even more so, all that He still has in store. Today, God calls you forward.

Today is just the beginning.

THE AUTHORS

Brittany Calavitta is an enthusiastic advocate for a good book, strong coffee, and a hopeful heart. She resides in Irvine, CA and is currently deep in the trenches of parenthood with her husband, David.

Leah Murphy is Life Teen's Coordinator of Digital Evangelization and Outreach. She's constantly looking for what's true, good, and beautiful in everything around her and has an insatiable desire for authenticity in all things. She's pursuing heaven on a messy little journey that Jesus is making beautiful, with new mercies every day.

Rachel Peñate will openly admit that she is a Wisconsin girl at heart and has a slight obsession with the band Switchfoot. Currently she resides in the beautiful, yet terribly hot Arizona desert, and serves as Assistant to the Executive Vice President of

Life Teen. When she is not managing book projects and writing her little heart out, she is hanging out with her two energetic dogs, husband Robbie, and daughter Cecilia.

Joel Stepanek has been actively and passionately involved in ministry for over ten years. Joel is the Director of Resource Development for Life Teen International where he creates engaging youth ministry resources for middle and high school students. Joel is an avid Packer fan (and owner), loves cooking, weightlifting, and spending time with his wife and two children, Elijah Daniel and Sophia Grace.

Jason Theobald is a youth minister at St. Mary's Parish in Huntley, IL. He lives with his wife Sarah and son Noah Michael in Sycamore, IL, where some of the greatest humans in the world are assembled. "There is no fear in love, but perfect love casts out all fear." 1 John 4:18.

LIFE TEEN
Leading Teens Closer to Christ
www.LifeTeen.com